what this sign-in book is all about

This sign-in book's for **you**. And for your friends, too. You can keep and cherish it forever. You and your friends can fill it with thoughts about life, likes, and love (among other things). It's the place to "speak out" and express yourself.

How this sign-in book works

Pass this sign-in book around to anyone and everyone you want to sign it (like your friends and classmates). A question appears at the top of every right-hand page — each person you pass the book to responds to each question. It can be fun to share and compare everyone's answers. Or you can keep it more private. Read on to find out how to start.

Each friend chooses and uses an identifying symbol or icon (like a heart or flower) instead of writing her name every time she answers a question. (*Sign-in city* is the place to record which name goes with which icon.)

Once you get started, you'll probably think up a bunch of questions you'd like to add to the ones already there. That's what the extra blank pages at the back of the book are for.

It's great to find out what everyone really thinks! Are you ready to speak out?

p.s. Not everyone filling out the book has to be a girl.

1

ISBN 0-439-16113-4

Copyright © 2000 by Scholastic Inc. All rights reserved.
Published by Scholastic Inc., 555 Broadway, New York, NY 10012.

Scholastic and associated logos are trademarks and/or registered trademarks of Scholastic Inc.

12 11 10 9 8 7 6 5 4 3 2   0 1 2 3 4 5/0

Printed in the U.S.A.   23

First Scholastic printing, January 2000

icon

name

sign-in city

icon	name

the most embarrassing experience of my entire life was when...

if i could meet any celebrity, i'd choose...(and say why!)

ONe thing i REAlly likE about my appEaRance is...

if i have a secret i want to keep, i definitely won't tell...

if i could have one wish come true, it would be...

if i could walk in someone else's shoes for a day, i'd choose...(why?)

my dEEp, daRk secREt is...

if i could chAnge my name, i'd chAnge it to...

oNe of thE things that reAlly reAlly boThErs mE is...

if i could go anywhere in the world, i'd go to...

if i were a cereal, the one i'd be is...